Creative
Bible Plays
For Kids

Kim D. Freeman

Creative Bible Plays For Kids

ISBN: 979-8-9918055-0-6 (ebook) 979-8-9918055-2-0 (Paperback)
979-8-9918055-3-7 (Hardcover)
Kim D. Freeman © 2024
All rights reserved.

Printed in the United States of America

Scriptures and references are from the King James Version of the Bible—public domain.

Contact information:

Email: kdfwellspring@gmail.com
Website: FreemanProductions-kim.net
YouTube Channel: @Kimfreeman306

Meet The Author

My name is Kim D. Freeman. I am a wife, a mom of three adult children, a sister, an aunt, a friend, an usher, a songwriter, a Children's Workshop Coordinator, and an author. I recently retired as a Registered Respiratory Therapist after working in the field for over 34 years. During my tenure, the Lord allowed me to assist in saving many people's lives. I love to sit with those who are in the later changes of life, and I plan to transition into chaplain training in the near future. The Lord is the head of my life, and I am not ashamed to share it.

My passion is service to people, especially, working with children between the ages of three and twelve. I desire to introduce them to Jesus Christ as their personal Savior at young ages so that they know a life based on foundational Biblical principles. Each play comes with helpful tips for success. The visual look presents lessons for applying God's Word. Children need to know that God is real and loves us with everlasting love. "For God so loved the world, that He gave His only begotten Son, that whosoever believeth in Him should not perish, but have everlasting life. For God sent not His Son into the world to condemn the world; but that the world through Him might be saved" (John 3:16, 17).

I write to visually show faith, healing, power, humility, and salvation. Some plays focus on David, Goliath, Joseph, humility, John the Baptist, miracles, and Jesus. I stepped away from ministry in 2016 to refresh. I was tired, frustrated, weak, and discouraged. The Lord renewed my strength through the Living Word. Now, I am ready to serve the Lord. I want to leave God's people with the hope that we all have a purpose and that we enhance our purpose when we align our spiritual gifts with those of our brothers and sisters.

Acknowledgments

Jesus Christ, my Lord, and Savior
Kelvin Freeman, my husband
The late Jack and Sharon Lyttle, my parents
Kelvin II, Kamille, and Kenneth, my children
Denise, Michelle, and Tanya, my sisters

The late Mr. & Mrs. Francis Freeman, my in-laws

My late Uncle Jack and Aunt Rose Ross, my family in New Castle
Mr. Sean-Anthony Roberts
Pastors, Apostle and Pastor Erica Sampson

To all children who supported this project

Tips For Success

1   Before each play, study the Scriptures about the basis of the play.

2   Give the children their lines at least two weeks before the first rehearsal. They will need to get familiar with their part.

3   If you choose to insert music, start to teach it at least two weeks before the first rehearsal. (It isn't easy to teach music and parts at the same rehearsal). Play music at every opportunity. Repetition is a great tool when communicating from one person to another. Insert songs wherever you see fit.

4   Perform a one-scene skit or a longer play depending on time.

5   Share costume ideas with those who are crafty in the congregation.

6   Design costumes that are easy to put on and take off.

7   Scan the Internet to observe people's costumes according to how people dressed in previous years. Please keep it simple.

8   Remember that the purpose of the plays is to preset a visual look of the Word of God.

9   Permit the children to customize the parts with new ideas, shorter lines, harmonization with music, or additional lines. Smile and keep it moving with creativity. This book is a starting guide for new ideas. For example, separate *When God Calls* into shorter plays.

10   Be creative and have fun!

11   Provide feedback to the author.

12   Not every child's production has the privilege of having a musician. This author provides music plus an instrumental for some selections.

Contents

Book 1

Open Our Open Eyes

Visual Experience of Open Our Open Eyes

Open Our Open Eyes is a play about our spiritual vision from Mark 1-10. Part One: Repent introduces the world to John the Baptist. He was the cousin and forerunner of Jesus Christ. John proclaimed repentance and the good news of the arrival of Jesus Christ. John baptized Jesus Christ in the Jordan River. The next day, he realized that Jesus was the Lamb of God who came to take away the sins of the world.

Part Two: Suffer the Little Children focuses on the vision of acceptance. Children came to see Jesus Christ, but the disciples rebuked those who brought the children to Jesus. As a result, Jesus Christ says it is okay for the children to come to Him, for such is the kingdom of God.

Part Three: Honor to Humility visualizes the desires of two brothers, James and John, the sons of Zebedee. Even though Jesus called them to be disciples, they had a problem. They desired to sit on the right and left of Jesus in glory, places of honor. Jesus said that the most critical place is the place of servanthood. There is a cost to the most excellent right and left places, and Jesus said the two brothers would get a taste of the price.

Part Four: Jesus traveled from Jerusalem to Jericho to open the eyes of a blind man named Bartimaeus, the son of Timeus. Bartimeus' physical eyes were closed, but his spiritual insight heard Jesus as He walked near Bartimeus. Blind Bartimaeus called out for Jesus to have mercy on him. Jesus healed Bartimaeus according to Bartimeus' faith.

Our eyes are open, but what do we see? After a visual adjustment, we may know that we are the ones to share the hope of repentance. Jesus said that children have value in His eyes. We may strive for high places, but the lower position prepares us for ministry. We overcome physical barriers with spiritual insight. May we allow the Holy Spirit to conquer the obstacles obstructing our spiritual vision. Amen!

Part One: Repent

Mark 1-Mark 9

Characters: John the Baptist, Person One, Person Two, Jesus, Dove, and Voice of God,

Props: Locusts, wild honey, camel blanket, and belt

Narrator: John the Baptist, Jesus' cousin, proclaims the good news of Jesus, the Son of God. He was a messenger. His message was straightforward and twofold: repent and look for the One, mightier than him. Repent means to turn away from sin. John the Baptist told others that Jesus was on the way.

(John the Baptist enters the room dressed in a camel blanket. He has two jars on his belt: one with locusts and one with wild honey. He walks around the room.)

John the Baptist: (Loudly) "The voice of one crying in the wilderness, Prepare ye the way of the Lord, Make his paths straight" (Mark 1:3). Repent, repent, repent!

John the Baptist: (Walking around) I am not worthy to untie the shoes of the one coming after me. Repent! Repent! Repent!

Person One: I repent!

John the Baptist: I will baptize you. (John baptizes Person One.)

Person Two: I repent!

John the Baptist: I will baptize you. (John baptizes Person Two.)

John the Baptist: Repent, repent, repent! "There cometh one mightier than I after me, the latchet of whose shoes I am not worthy to stoop down and unloose. I indeed have baptized you with water: but He shall baptize you with the Holy Ghost" (Mark 1:7-8).

John the Baptist: Repent! Repent! Repent!

(Jesus walks in. John baptizes Jesus.)

Dove: (A dove rests on Jesus after the baptism.) (Mark 1:10)

Voice of God: "Thou art my beloved Son, in whom I am well pleased" (Mark 1:11).

(Everyone leaves except for Jesus.)

Jesus: "The time is fulfilled, and the kingdom of God is at hand: repent ye, and believe the gospel" (Mark 1:15). The Son of man came to open the eyes of those who are lost. The Son of man called twelve disciples cast out unclean spirits, healed a man with leprosy, and healed a paralyzed man. The Son of man ate with sinners, healed on the Sabbath, taught from parables, calmed the storm, raised a little girl from the dead, fed thousands of people, walked on water, healed a deaf and mute man, and healed a blind man. The Son of man came to open the eyes of the blind! The Son of man will be seen by many, suffer many things, be rejected by many, be killed, and after three days, rise again. Repent and believe the gospel!

(Everyone leaves.)

♫ *Repent and Be Baptized* ♫

I've come with a message today. A message of hope to live every day.
Open our open eyes. Repent and be baptized.
The message is simple. The message is right.
Repent and be baptized.

I've come with a message today. A message of hope to live every day.
Open our open eyes. Repent and be baptized.
The message is simple. The message is right.
Repent and be baptized.

I've come with a message today. A message of hope to live every day.
Open our open eyes. Repent and be baptized.
The message is simple. The message is right.
Repent and be baptized.

Open our open eyes. Repent and be baptized.
The message is simple. The message is right.
Repent and be baptized.

End of Part One

Part Two: Suffer the Little Children

Mark 10:13-16

Characters: Narrator, an adult, three children, Jesus, James, and John

Props: Games, fun activities

Narrator: In preparation for his work, Jesus made it a point to focus on children. He welcomed the children. This scene takes us back to when people brought the children to Jesus. This scene introduces music, games, and greetings by Jesus. The disciples decided to rebuke those who brought the children to Jesus. Jesus said that the children are welcome to come to Him. Jesus opened the eyes of those who criticized the presence of the children.

(Jesus sits in a chair in the corner of the room. The band plays music)

Child #1: Hi, Jesus! (unique handshake, gives Jesus a high five).

Jesus: Hello.

Child # 2: Hi, Jesus! (unique handshake gives a high-five).

Jesus: Hello.

Child # 3: Hi, Jesus! (unique handshake gives a high five).

Jesus: Hello.

(Music plays and the little children gather around Jesus and clap to the music).

James & John: (running in toward the children) We rebuke you for bringing your children around here! (Mark 10:13)

All children: Jesus said that we could come.

Jesus: (standing up) "Suffer the little children to come unto me, and forbid them not: for of such is the kingdom of God. Verily I say unto you, Whosoever shall not receive the kingdom of God as a little child, he shall not enter therein" (Mark 10:14-15).

(All children gather around Jesus as they leave.)

♫*Open Our Eyes*♫

Psalm 119:18

Open our eyes to the things before us. Open our eyes to the ways that you move. Open our eyes so that we do not miss you, for you are speaking a word in us. (repeat)

Come into the service. Touch this one and that. Move all through the pews from the front to the back. Anoint us and make us a sight to behold. Open our eyes, Lord. (Repeat)

Open our eyes. Open our eyes. Open our eyes. Open our eyes.
Open our eyes. Open our eyes. Open our eyes. Open our eyes.

Psalm 119:18 says, Open thou mine eyes that I behold wondrous things out of thy law.

Open our eyes, open our eyes, open our eyes. Open our eyes.
Open our eyes, open our eyes, open our eyes. Open our eyes.
Open our eyes. Open our eyes. Open my eyes, Father.

End of Part Two

Part Three: Honor to Humility

Mark 10:35-45

Characters: Narrator, James, John, Jesus

Props: Two king-like outfits

Narrator: Scene three focuses on two brothers, the sons of Zebedee. Even though Jesus called them to be disciples, they had a problem. They desired to sit on the right and left of Jesus in glory, places of honor. Jesus said that the most critical place is the place of servanthood. There is a cost to the most excellent right and left places, and Jesus said that the two brothers would get a taste of the cost of humility.

(James and John in the center of the stage.)

John: James, I was thinking about something. Maybe I can sit on Jesus' right side in glory. (He wears fancy clothes). This is my honor outfit!

James: John, if you are on the right, I will be on the left in glory. This is my honor outfit. I can practice looking the part (He puts on fancy clothes).

♫ *Right-Left* ♫

When we get to glory, I'll be on the right.
When we get to glory, I'll be on the left.
Right-left, right-left, I so desire on the right or the left. (repeat)

I desire a place of honor. I desire a place for me.
I desire that others will see Jesus honoring me.

When we get to glory, I'll be on the right.
When we get to glory, I'll be on the left.
Right-left, right-left, I so desire on the right or the left.

I desire a place of honor. I desire a place for me.
I desire that others will see Jesus honoring me.

When we get to glory, I'll be on the right.
When we get to glory, I'll be on the left.
Right-left, right-left, I so desire on the right or the left.

Right-left, right-left, I so desire on the right or the left.
Right-left, right-left, I so desire on the right or the left.

(Jesus walks in.)

James: Hi, Jesus!

John: I was thinking about you.

Jesus: We will go to Jerusalem. The Son of man will be delivered to the chief priest and the scribes. Some will mock and condemn death, but the Son of man will rise again. They told him what they were thinking, but what were you thinking? (Mark 10:33-34)

John: Well, Master, I desire to sit on your right side in glory. (Mark 10:37)

James: Master, I desire to sit in glory on your left side. (Mark 10:37)

Jesus: Do you realize what you are asking? Are you willing to drink from my cup and receive my baptism? (Mark 10:38)

James & John: (With excitement) Yes! (Mark 10:39)

Jesus: You WILL drink of my cup and experience my baptism, but the right and left seats are not mine to give. The greatest one shall be the servant of all. The Son of man came to serve and give his life as a ransom for many. (Mark 10:39-45)

<h1 style="text-align:center">♫ My Hands Are Out ♫</h1>

Psalm 24:4

My hands are out. My heart is pure. I came to serve forever more.
No right or left. No left or right. My eyes will be open tonight.

My hands are out. My heart is pure. I came to serve forever more.
No right or left. No left or right. My eyes will be open tonight.

My hands are out. My heart is pure. I came to serve forever more.
No right or left. No left or right. My eyes will be open tonight.

Hallelujah, Hallelujah, Hallelujah, Hallelujah
Hallelujah, Hallelujah, Hallelujah, Hallelujah

The Lord's Prayer

End of Part Three

Part Four: Blind Bartimaeus, the son of Timaeus

Mark 10:46-52

Characters: Narrator: Two people, James, John, and Blind Bartimaeus

Props: Beggers cups, sunglasses, cloak

Narrator: There was a blind man named Bartimaeus in Mark 10:46-52. He had spiritual insight into the healing power of Jesus, but he lacked physical sight. Jesus traveled from Jerusalem to Jericho to open the physical eyes of a blind man named Bartimaeus, the son of Timeus. Bartimaeus heard Jesus as he walked near Bartimeus. Jesus healed Bartimaeus according to Bartimeus' faith.

(A blind man carries his garment and cup onto the stage.)

Bartimeus: (holding out the cup) Help me, anyone! I am a beggar!

Person #1: (Walking in)

Bartimeus: (Holding the cup out) Help me, anyone. I am a beggar!

Person #1: Be quiet, Bartimaeus! (Person leaves)

Person #2: (Walking in)

Bartimeus: (Holding the cup out) Help me, anyone. I am a beggar!

Person #2: Be quiet, Bartimaeus!

(Person leaves. Jesus walks in with James and John.)

Bartimeus: I hear Jesus coming! Jesus, thou Son of David, have mercy on me!

Person 1 & 2: Be quiet, Bartimaeus!

Bartimeus: (louder) Thou Son of David, have mercy on me!

Person 1 & 2: Be quiet, Bartimaeus!

Bartimeus: (Even louder) Thou Son of David, have mercy on me!

Jesus: (Standing still) Call that man.

James and John: (Walking to the man) Be of good cheer. Jesus is calling you (Mark 10:49)

Bartimeus: (Throwing his garment and walking to Jesus) (Mark 10:50)

Jesus: What can I do for you? (Mark 10:51)

Bartimeus: Lord, I want to see! (Mark 10:51)

Jesus: Go your way. Your faith has made you whole. (Mark 10:52)

Narrator: Jesus predicted His death, but He rose again with all power. He has risen! John the Baptist said to repent. Jesus said to repent. Who will tell the message of repentance and allow the Lord to open our open eyes? The children are here to say it! Repent and believe. Open your open eyes!

♫Jesus, I Want To See ♫

Mark 10:51

Help me to see which way I should go which way I should go I just do not know. Help me to see which way I should go. Jesus, I want to see. Jesus, I want to see. (Repeat)

I want to see the One who had mercy on me. I want to see the One who will heal me. See the One who will open up my eyes. Jesus, I want to see. Jesus, I want to see.

Help me to see which way I should go which way I should go I just do not know. Help me to see which way I should go. Jesus, I want to see. Jesus, I want to see.

I want to see the One who had mercy on me. I want to see the One who will heal me. See the One who will open up my eyes. Jesus, I want to see. Jesus, I want to see. (Repeat)

The End

Book 2

David and Goliath Revised Edition

Visual Experience of David and Goliath

Kim Freeman Productions emphasizes a visual experience for all participants. The first visual experience from *David and Goliath* is that children are not too young to answer God's call. David was the youngest of the brothers. When Samuel came to anoint the next king, the father did not mention David as a top choice until Samuel asked if Jesse had more sons. After God's approval, Samuel anointed David as a child in the presence of his father and brothers.

The second visual experience is that children are not too young to worship. David created an atmosphere of worship while he tended to the sheep. David wrote psalms that reflected his relationship with the Lord. David loved the Lord, and the Lord loved David.

The third visual experience is that children are not too young to have faith. David killed a lion and a bear when they attempted to take his sheep. David trusted the Lord in personal battles. Since David had faith in previous victories, he had faith in the Lord's ability to provide the power to defeat Goliath.

The fourth visual experience is that children are not too young to experience salvation. One way to verbalize faith is by confessing Jesus Christ as personal Savior. "That if thou shalt confess with thy mouth the Lord Jesus, and shalt believe in thine heart that God hath raised him from the dead, thou shalt be saved. For with the heart man believeth unto righteousness; and with the mouth confession is made unto salvation" (Romans 10:9-10). Enjoy!

Part One: Children are not too young to answer God's call.

I Samuel 16:1-13, I Samuel 17:34-36

Characters: Voice of God, Narrator, David, Nathan, Jesse, Samuel, Four Levitical Priests, seven sons of Jesse, sheep, lion, bear, and a messenger

Props: chair, rag, anointing oil, sheepfold, paper, pen, and slingshot

(The scene opens with Samuel the Prophet standing at center stage.)

Narrator: David was a shepherd who cared for sheep. God called David at a young age to be his choice as the king of Israel. Samuel the Prophet anointed David for his calling as king among his father and brothers. Although he did not become king until years later, David obeyed God's call. David loved to praise the Lord. When David sinned, he asked for forgiveness and still praised the Lord. God established His kingdom through the line of David for His kingdom to last forever.

(Samuel enters the stage. He looks sad.)

Voice of God: "How long will you mourn for Saul, seeing I have rejected him from reigning over Israel? Fill thy horn with oil, and go, I send you to Jesse the Bethlehemite: for I have provided me a king among his sons" (1 Samuel 16:1).

Samuel: Saul will not like this of me (1 Samuel 16:2).

Voice of God: Samuel, go, and sacrifice to the Lord (1 Samuel 16:2).

(Samuel leaves. Jesse enters and cleans around the stage.) (Samuel knocks, and Jesse answers the door. They talk.)

Jesse: Samuel, did you come in peace? (1 Samuel 16:4)

Samuel: I come to you in peace. The Lord sent me here today to anoint the next king of Israel among one of your sons (1 Samuel 16:4-5).

Jesse: Look at my first son, Eliab. (Eliab walks to Samuel.) (1 Samuel 16:6)

Samuel: Surely, the Lord's anointed is before me. (1 Samuel 16:6).

Voice of God: "Look not on his countenance or on the height of his stature, because I refused him: for the Lord sees not as man sees; for man looks at the outward appearance, but the Lord looks at the heart." (1 Samuel 16:7).

(The other sons pass before Samuel, but he does not show approval.)

Samuel: (Looking at Jesse) Do you have any other children? (1 Samuel 16:11b)

Jesse: There is the youngest. He is with the sheep (1 Samuel 16:11c).

Samuel: Go get him! (1 Samuel 16:11d). (The scene moves to David with his sheep.)

Narrator: David writes a psalm in the field as he tends to the sheep.

David: Thank you, Lord, for such a beautiful day. Sheep, are you there?

Sheep: Baa, baa, baa!

David: (Excited) All right! Good sheep! Call me if you hear any danger.

Sheep: Baa, baa, baa!

(David writes on paper and then falls asleep.)

Lion: (A lion steps over David. The lion takes a sheep and runs with the sheep.)

Sheep: Baa, baa, baa!

David: (David uses a slingshot to aim at the lion. The lion falls. David recovers his sheep.) "The Lord is my light and my salvation; whom shall I fear? The Lord is the strength of my life; of whom shall I be afraid?" (Psalm 23:1)

Sheep: Baa, baa, baa!

David: (Excited) All right! Good sheep! Call me if you hear any danger.

Sheep: Baa, baa, baa!

(David writes on paper and then falls asleep.)

Lion: (A bear steps over David. The bear takes a sheep and runs with the sheep.)

Sheep: Baa, baa, baa!

David: (David uses a slingshot to aim at the bear. The bear falls. David recovers his sheep.) "The Lord is my light and my salvation;

whom shall I fear? The Lord is the strength of my life; of whom shall I be afraid?" (Psalm 23:1)

Messenger: David, your father wants you. I will stay with the sheep.

(David joins his father and brothers.)

Voice of God: "Arise, anoint him: for this is he" (1 Samuel 16:13). (Samuel anoints David among his father and brothers. Everyone exits.)

♫ *Song-I Am a Promise of God* ♫

Galatians 3:26-29

God cares about His promises.
God cares. He said in His word.
God cares about His promises.
I am a promise of God.

God cares about His promises.
God cares. He said in His word.
God cares about His promises.
I am a promise of God.

I am an heir, joint heirs with Jesus.
An heir; I am a promise.
An heir; Abraham's seed.
I am a promise of God.

I am an heir, joint heirs with Jesus.
An heir; I am a promise.
An heir; Abraham's seed.
I am a promise of God. Yes, I am a promise of God.

I am, I am a promise. I am, I am a promise of God.
I am, I am a promise. I am, I am a promise of God.
I am, I am a promise. I am, I am a promise of God.
I am, I am a promise.

I am a promise of God. Yes, I am a promise of God.
Yes, I am a promise of God.

End of Part One

Part Two: Children are not too young to worship.

1 Samuel 16:14-23

Characters: David, three servants, King Saul

Props: Harp, chair, and pillow

Narrator: This scene opens with an angry King Saul pacing back and forth. He kicks a pillow across the stage. David plays an instrument for King Saul, and the spirit departs from King Saul.

First Servant: Dear King Saul, I see that you are troubled! Can I help?

King Saul: (Pacing) I am troubled by a spirit. (1 Samuel 16:14-16)

Second Servant: Dear King Saul, you are troubled!

King Saul: (Pacing) I know that!

Third Servant: Dear King Saul, you are troubled!

King Saul: (Pacing) I would like to hear from someone skillful on the harp! (1 Samuel16:16)

All Servants: The son of Jesse plays very well! (1 Samuel 16:17)

King Saul: (Pacing) Send a message to Jesse to get David to play for me! (1 Samuel 16:18)

(The servants leave and return with David.)

David: (David has a harp and plays it. King Saul slows his pace until he finally falls asleep while David plays the harp.)

(They all leave.)

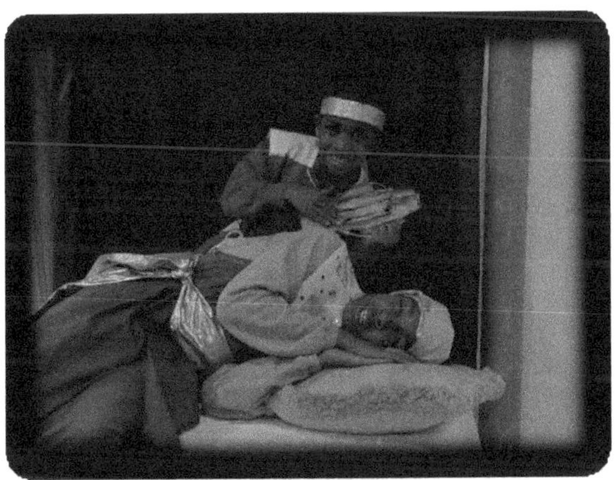

♫ *At The Name of Jesus* ♫

Isaiah 45:23-24; Philippians 2:5-11.

At the name of Jesus, every knee shall bow.
At the name of Jesus, every knee shall bow.
At His name, the enemy trembles.
At His name, sick bodies are healed.
At the name of Jesus, every knee shall bow. Every knee shall bow.

The name of Jesus is holy and precious.
He's more than precious to me.
He is so great, the Son of the Highest.
He rules and reigns as our King.
His name is above every name. All things are under His feet.
Come bow your knees and worship Him. Worship the Holy King at His name.

At the name of Jesus, every knee shall bow.
At the name of Jesus, every knee shall bow.
At His name, the enemy trembles
At His name, sick bodies are healed.
At the name of Jesus, every knee shall bow. Every knee shall bow.

At I'm gonna call on Jesus. At I'm gonna call on Jesus.
At I'm gonna call on Jesus. At I'm gonna call on Jesus.

At I said the enemy trembles. At I said the enemy trembles.
At I said the enemy trembles. At I said the enemy trembles.

At Jesus, Jesus, Jesus. At Jesus, Jesus, Jesus.
At Jesus, Jesus, Jesus. At Jesus, Jesus, Jesus.
At the name of Jesus

Every knee shall bow. Every knee shall bow. Every knee shall bow.

End of part two.

Part Three: Children are not too young to have faith.

1 Samuel 17:1-51

Characters: David and Goliath

Props: Slingshot

Narrator: It was time for war with the Israelites against the Philistines. The Israelites camped on the hill north of the Elah Valley, and the Philistines camped on the hill south of the Elah Valley. Goliath challenged someone to fight him for 40 days. No one, including King Saul or David's brothers, stood up for the challenge. David came along and stood victorious against the giant.

Goliath: I am a Philistine. "I defy the armies of Israel this day; give me a man, that we may fight together" (1 Samuel 17:10).

(David walks in.)

Goliath: I am a Philistine. "I defy the armies of Israel this day; give me a man, that we may fight together" (1 Samuel 17:10).

David: Brothers, who is that?

Brother: He is Goliath of Gath. He is a Philistine. He wants to fight one of us. If we win, they will serve us. If he wins, we will serve them (1 Samuel 17:25).

King Saul: You are too young! (1 Samuel 17:33)

David: (With Confidence) I killed the lion and the bear. This Philistine defies the armies of the living God! (1 Samuel 17:35-37)

King Saul: Wear my armor (1 Samuel 17:38).

David: I have not proved your armor (1 Samuel 17:39).

Goliath: (Looking at David) Am I a dog that you come to me with sticks? (1 Samuel 17:43) I will give your body to the fowls of the air and the beasts of the field (1 Samuel 17:44).

David: You come with a sword, spear, and shield, but I come in the name of the Lord of hosts (1 Samuel 17:45). The battle is the Lord's. (David aims his slingshot at Goliath, and he falls. David rejoices.)

Narrator: David spent time in God's Word before he faced life's challenges. He was victorious. Children face various challenges in life. The Lord is not asleep. He desires us to call upon Him in a time of need. He wants our time and our attention toward Him. During those times, He reassures us that He calls us for service, our worship is valuable, age does not matter, and we are victorious through Him.

♫ *Step of Faith* ♫

2 Corinthians 5:7; Philippians 3:14

I'm taking a step of faith. I'm walking with the Lord.
I can't see my way around. I'll put one foot on the ground.
I press toward the mark above. It's full steam ahead.
I'm on my way. I'm moving ahead. I'm moving ahead.

I'm taking a step, a step of faith.
The power of God is my life. I'm moving ahead.
I'm taking a step, a step of faith.
The power of God is my life. I'm moving ahead.

I'm taking a step of faith. I'm walking with the Lord.
I can't see my way around. I'll put one foot on the ground.
I press toward the mark above. It's full steam ahead.
I'm on my way. I'm moving ahead. I'm moving ahead.

I'm taking a step, a step of faith.
The power of God is my life. I'm moving ahead. I'm taking a step, a step of faith.
The power of God is my life, I'm moving ahead.

Nothing can stop me. Nothing can block me.
I'm on my way now, a step of faith.
Nothing can stop me. Nothing can block me.
I'm on my way now.

The power of God is in my life. I'm moving ahead.
The power of God is in my life. I'm moving ahead.
The power of God is in my life. I'm moving ahead.

33

End of part three

Part Four:

Children are not too young to know about salvation.

Jesus Christ, the Son of God, is the Savior of the world. He gave His life for us. Therefore, one way to demonstrate faith is by accepting Jesus Christ as personal Savior. "For God so loved the world that He gave His only begotten Son, that whosoever believeth in Him should not perish, but have everlasting life. For God sent not His Son into the world to condemn the world; but that the world through Him might be saved" (John 3:16-17).

Another way to demonstrate faith is by believing God raised Jesus Christ from the dead. Jesus Christ took the sin of the world upon His shoulders, and He died in our place so that we would have a right to eternal life. The faith part is that Jesus Christ sacrificed His life for imperfect people. His love is so great that He freely presents Himself as a ransom for our sins according to grace. "For by grace are ye saved through faith: and that not of yourselves: it is a gift of God: Not of works, lest any man should boast" (Ephesians 2:8-

9).

One way to verbalize faith is by confessing Jesus Christ as personal Savior. "That if thou shalt confess with thy mouth the Lord Jesus, and shalt believe in thine heart that God hath raised him from the dead, thou shalt be saved. For with the heart man believeth unto righteousness; and with the mouth confession is made unto salvation" (Romans 10:9-10).

♫ *The Way* ♫

John 14:6

He is the way, the truth, the life, the way.
He is the way, the truth, the life, the way.
He is the way, the truth, the life, the way.
He is the way, the truth, the life, the way.
He is the way, the truth, the life, the way.
He is the way, the truth, the life, the way.
He is the way, the truth, the life, the way.
He is the way, the truth, the life, the way.
John 14:1-6

The End

Book 3

Miracles

A Visual Experience of Miracles

Miracles and healings take place throughout the Bible. The Book of St. John contains many miracles to grip readers' attention. Jesus healed according to faith, according to His word and will, and according to a touch. Jesus did not touch everyone that He healed. Some experienced healing from their faith alone, some followed Jesus' directions, and some did unusual things.

A miracle happened when Jesus healed a nobleman's son. A father asked Jesus to heal his son. Jesus spoke the word of healing. The father believed Jesus, and the son received his healing. Another miracle occurred at a pool when Jesus healed a paralyzed man. The man obeyed the words of Jesus and received his healing when he followed Jesus' commands. Yet, another miracle occurred when Jesus healed a woman of her 12-year issue of blood according to her faith. The Bible did not say that Jesus touched them with His hands during the three healings, but he healed all of them.

Along with the miracles, a woman thought enough of Jesus to anoint His body for burial amid the presence of others. Amid a group, a woman poured perfume on Jesus' head. She wiped His feet with her hair. She sacrificed the most precious thing in her possession, the alabaster oil, while Jesus sacrificed the most precious thing He had, which was His life.

John 20:30-31 says, "And many other signs truly did Jesus in the presence of His disciples, which are not written in this book: But these are written, that ye might believe that Jesus is the Christ, the Son of God; and that believing ye might have life through His name."

Part One: Jesus Heals the Nobleman's Son

John 4:43-54

Characters: Narrator, Jesus, Two Disciples, Nobleman, Wife, Son, and Two Servants

Props: Bed

Narrator: The first miracle occurred when Jesus turned water into wine at a wedding. The second miracle happened when Jesus healed a nobleman's son. A nobleman in the Bible had a sick son at Capernaum. Knowing that his son was at the point of death created urgency for the nobleman to seek Jesus. He knew that Jesus healed others, so he desired a healing for his son. The nobleman greets Jesus with his concern. Jesus heals his son, and the whole house believes in Jesus.

(Jesus is at the center with a few disciples.)

Nobleman: (Running toward Jesus) Please come and heal my son. He is at the point of death! (John 4:47)

Jesus: "Except ye see signs and wonders, ye will not believe" (John 4:48).

Nobleman: Sir, come down before my son dies (John 4:49).

Jesus: Go thy way; thy son lives (John 4:50a).

Nobleman: I believe! (John 4:50)

(He leaves. The servants meet him before he goes home).

Servants: (Running toward Nobleman) Your son lives! (John 4:51)

Nobleman: What time did my son feel better? (John 4:52) **Servants:** Yesterday at the seventh hour (John 4:52).

Nobleman: That was the same hour that Jesus spoke it! (John 4:53).

Wife: I believe! (John 4:53)

Son: (Getting up from his bed) I believe! (John 4:53)

Servants: We believe! (Everyone leaves.)

♫ *Surely the Presence of the Lord is in This Place* ♫

Acts 2:1-4

Surely the presence of the Lord is in this place.
I can feel His mighty power and His grace.
I can hear the brush of angel's wings. I see glory on each face.
Surely the presence of the Lord is in this place.

In the midst of His children, the Lord said He would be.
It doesn't take very many it can be just two or three.
And I feel that same sweet Spirit that I felt oft times before.
Surely, I can say I've been with the Lord.

Surely the presence of the Lord is in this place. I can feel
His mighty power and His grace.
I can hear the brush of angels' wings. I see glory on each face.
Surely the presence of the Lord is in this place.

There's a holy hush around us as God's glory fills this place.
I've touched the hem of His garment I can almost see His face.
And my heart is overflowing with the fullness of His joy.
I know without a doubt that I've been with the Lord.

End of Part One

Part Two: Jesus Heals the Paralyzed Man

John 5:1-9

Characters: Narrator, Jesus, a Man

Props: Bed, pool, and sound effects of water

Narrator: The book of John shares a miracle about how Jesus healed a paralyzed man at the pool of Bethesda. When an angel troubled the water, the first person in the water received a healing. The man, lying at the pool for 38 years, converses with Jesus about his condition. Jesus healed the man when the man obeyed the words of Jesus.

Jesus: (Walking to the man) Do you want to be whole? (John 5:6b)

Man: (Laying by the pool) I don't have anyone to put me into the water. When the troubling of the water occurs, someone steps in the water before me (John 4:7).

Jesus: Rise, take up your bed, and walk! (John 5:8)

Man: (The man gets up, takes his bed, and walks. (John 5:9).

♫ *Step of Faith* ♫

2 Corinthians 5:7 and Philippians 3:14

I'm taking a step of faith. I'm walking with the Lord.
I can't see my way around. I'll put one foot on the ground.
I press toward the mark above. It's full steam ahead.
I'm on my way. I'm moving ahead. I'm moving ahead.

I'm taking a step, a step of faith.
The power of God is my life. I'm moving ahead.
I'm taking a step, a step of faith.
The power of God is my life. I'm moving ahead.

I'm taking a step of faith. I'm walking with the Lord.
I can't see my way around. I'll put one foot on the ground.
I press toward the mark above. It's full steam ahead.
I'm on my way. I'm moving ahead. I'm moving ahead.

I'm taking a step, a step of faith.
The power of God is my life. I'm moving ahead.
I'm taking a step, a step of faith.
The power of God is my life. I'm moving ahead.

Nothing can stop me. Nothing can block me.
I'm on my way now, a step of faith.
Nothing can stop me. Nothing can block me.
I'm on my way now.

The power of God is in my life. I'm moving ahead.
The power of God is in my life. I'm moving ahead.
The power of God is in my life. I'm moving ahead.

End of Part Two

Part Three. Jesus Heals a Woman with an Issue of Blood

Characters: Narrator, Person One, Person Two, Woman, Jesus, and Crowd

Props: Red Robe or Scarf wrapped around the woman

Narrator: Mark 5:25-28 says, "And a certain woman, which had an issue of blood twelve years, and had suffered many things of many physicians, and had spent all that she had, and was nothing bettered, but rather grew worse. When she had heard of Jesus, came in the press behind, and touched His garment. For she said, if I may touch but His clothes, I shall be whole." Jesus healed her according to her faith.

(Jesus enters with a crowd.)

Member One: There are so many people who want to see Jesus!

Member Two: I know! That woman has been trying to get to Jesus!

Woman: (Pushing through the crowd) Let me get through to get to Jesus! I have an issue, and only Jesus can heal me! I need to touch His clothes! (Mark 5:27)

Crowd: (The crowd gets in the way.)

Woman: If I could touch His clothes, I would be made whole! (She touches Jesus' hem of the garment.) (Mark 5:28)

Jesus: (Stopping, turning around quickly) Who touched me? (Mark 5:31)

Members One, Member Two, and Crowd: Jesus we all touched you! (Mark 5:31)

Jesus: (Looking around) This touch was different! Virtue left me (Mark 5:31-32).

Woman: (On her knees) I touched you (Mark 5:33).

Jesus: Daughter, your faith has made you whole. Go in peace (Mark 5:34)

(The woman rejoices as they leave.)

♫ *Just One Touch*♫

Matthew 9:20-22; Mark 5:25-34; and Luke 8:43-48.

Just one touch from the Master's hand, and I know I'll be made whole. Just one touch from the Master's hand, and I know I'll be made whole. I know I'll be made whole.

Just one touch from the Master's hand, and I know I'll be made whole. Just one touch from the Master's hand, and I know I'll be made whole. I know I'll be made whole.

The Bible tells us about a woman with an issue.
She had an issue for twelve long years.
She knew if she could just get to Jesus.
She would be whole and cry no more tears.
She pressed her way to get to the Master.
She touched his clothes and knew she was healed.
The Master said your faith has healed you. You are whole now go in peace.

Just one touch from the Master's hand, and I know I'll be made whole. Just one touch from the Master's hand, and I know I'll be made whole. I know I'll be made whole.

Gonna press my way to get to the Master.
Gonna press my way through all obstacles.
Gonna press my way. Nothing can stop me.
I know I'll be made whole. I know I'll be made whole.

Just one touch from the Master's hand, and I know I'll be made whole. Just one touch from the Master's hand, and I know I'll be made whole. I know I'll be made whole.

He touched me. The Master touched me.
He touched me. The Master touched me. Now I am whole.

He touched me. The Master touched me.
He touched me. the Master touched me. Now I am whole.
He touched me. The Master touched me.
He touched me. The Master touched me. Now I am whole.
He touched me. The Master touched me.
He touched me. The Master touched me. Now I am whole.

End of Part Three

Part Four: A Woman Anoints Jesus

Characters: Narrator, Jesus, Simon the leper, Disciple, Woman

Props: Table, Perfume bottle, and long-haired wig for the woman

Narrator: A woman anoints Jesus. "And being in Bethany in the house of Simon the leper, as he sat at meat, there came a woman having an alabaster box of ointment of spikenard very precious; and she brake the box, and poured it on his head" (Mark 14:3). There were some in the company that did not agree with the manner of Jesus' anointing by the woman. Jesus said that the woman anointed Him for His burial.

(Everyone gathers around at a dinner table.)

Jesus: Thank you, Simon, for the dinner.

Disciple: The meal was terrific!

Woman: (The woman enters the room. She opens the perfume. She pours it on Jesus' head. She washes His feet with her hair (Mark 14:3).

Disciple: (With anger) Woman, you wasted this expensive oil! That oil could have been sold to help the poor! (Mark 14:4-5)

Jesus: Let her alone. She did someone good. You will always have the poor, but I will not always be here. She anointed my body for my burial. She will be remembered for this (Mark 14:6-9).

Woman: (She continues to anoint Jesus during the song.)

♫ *Pour the Oil* ♫

Matthew 26:6-13; Mark 14:3-9; Luke 7:36-50; John 12:1-8.

As the woman poured oil, costly oil, she said not a mumbling word.
As she came to Jesus, she poured the oil
From His head down to His feet.
The disciple said woman you wasted the oil.
You wasted it for no cause.
But when Jesus heard them refer to the oil, this is just what He said: I've been
anointed to die for you. The woman saw no waste.
She poured from my head to my feet.
The poor you have always but Me as your Savior,
I've been anointed to die for you. I've been anointed to die for you.

As the woman poured oil, costly oil, she said not a mumbling word. As she came
to Jesus, she poured the oil
From His head down to His feet.
The disciple said woman you wasted the oil. You wasted it for no cause.
But when Jesus heard them refer to the oil, this is just what He said: I've been
anointed to die for you. The woman saw no waste.
She poured from My head to My feet.
The poor you have always but Me as your Savior,
I've been anointed to die for you. I've been anointed to die for you.

Pour the oil, the alabaster oil. Pour the oil, the alabaster oil.
Pour the oil, the alabaster oil. Pour the oil, the alabaster oil.
From my head to my feet Pour, pour it pour it on him, the alabaster oil
From my head to my feet Pour, pour it pour it on him, the alabaster oil
From my head to my feet Pour, pour it pour it on him, the alabaster oil
From my head to my feet Pour, pour it pour it on him, the alabaster oil
From my head to my feet

The End

Book 4

The Making of the Humility Sandwich Revised Edition

Visual Experience of The Making of the Humility Sandwich

The Chief Chef, who wears all white, is in charge. They give each cast member a special ingredient for building the humility sandwich. Each component has Scriptures from Philippians 2:5-11 and Hebrews 9:22. Red Ralph is a dancer. When Red Ralph hears the word "blood," he dances for a while.

Each cast member wears an apron and an accompanying chef's hat, coordinating with the letter of their ingredients. For example, Red Ralph is "C," Orange Orin is "H," Yellow Yvonne "O," Green Gus is "S," Blue Betty is "E," and Purple Paul is "N." The ingredient spells the word C.H.O.S.E.N. Have fun!

What a fun play! The children loved it! They laughed, giggled, and related to how a common task of making a sandwich created an avenue of remembering the Scriptures related to the humility of Jesus Christ. The recipe book is the Bible, and the process of humility reminds us to remain humble in everything that we do.

Part One: "C" and "H"

Characters: All Chefs and Two Volunteers

Props: A long table or two short tables, seven plates, seven aprons, seven chef's hats, seven pairs of gloves, a basin for foot washing, and a towel

(All cast members enter and gather around the table in order (Ralph, Orin, Yvonne, Gus, Betty, Purple).

Chief Chef: Thank you, and good morning! I am the Chief Chef. I am here to instruct my fellow chefs on *The Making of the Humility Sandwich.* Today, we will use an old family recipe in Philippians 2:5-11 and Hebrews 9:22. Follow along in your Bibles as I teach my fellow chefs about humility.

All Chefs: (Looking surprised) The humility sandwich?

Chief Chef: Yes, the humility sandwich!

Red Ralph: Chief Chef, I don't mind learning about the humility sandwich, but I don't want to see or hear the word "blood" unless I have room to dance.

Chief Chef: Don't worry! We will step aside and give you room to dance when we say the word "blood." (Pause) All chefs, first, we must wash our hands.

(They all pretend to wash their hands. They put gloves on.)

Chief Chef: Red Ralph, you have the first ingredient.

Red Ralph: The first ingredient for our humility sandwich begins with the letter "C." The first ingredient is "Christ." "Let this mind be in you which was also in Christ Jesus: Who, being in the form of God, thought it not robbery to be equal with God" (Philippians 2:5-6).

Chief Chef: Fellow chefs, place the "C" on our humility sandwich. He is the foundation of the sandwich.

(Everyone takes their "C," lifts it high in the air, and places it on each person's plate.)

Orange Orin: Our second ingredient for our humility sandwich begins with the letter "H." The ingredient is "Himself." "But made Himself of no reputation, and took upon Him the form of a servant, and was made in the likeness of men" (Philippians 2:7). (Sentimentally) Whenever I hear the word Himself, I think of servanthood. I feel the need to wash the feet of others like Jesus did.

All Chefs: Yuck! (Holding their noses) Who wants to serve by washing the feet of others?

Chief Chef: He is right! Jesus washed the feet of His disciples. We must follow all instructions to complete this lesson, not just the fun ones.

Orange Orin: Any volunteers?

Volunteer: (Standing) I'll do it!

Another Volunteer: (Standing) I will also do it!

Orange Orin: (He washed the feet of both volunteers.)

Chief Chef: Fellow chefs, place the "H" as a servant on our humility sandwich.

(Everyone takes their "H," lifts it high in the air, and places it on each person's plate.)

Orange Orin: Here is a song to feed our minds. We must serve like Christ.

♫ *This is the Time to Celebrate* ♫

Part One
This is the time to celebrate.
This is the time to celebrate.
This is the time to celebrate Jesus, our king.

This is the time to celebrate.
This is the time to celebrate.
This is the time to celebrate Jesus, our king.

Part Two
We're going to adore for He's wonderful, and He is the mighty God.
Bow down before Him as the king of kings. I will give Him my all.
He's Alpha and Omega. He is the first, and He is the very last.
He is my Savior. He is my friend. He has washed me from my past.

We're going to adore for He's wonderful, and He is the mighty God.
Bow down before Him as the king of kings. I will give Him my all.
He's Alpha and Omega. He is the first, and He is the very last.
He is my Savior. He is my friend. He has washed me from my past.

Part Three
This is the time to Hallelujah. This is the time to celebrate.
This is the time to Hallelujah. Jesus, our king.

This is the time to Hallelujah. This is the time to celebrate.
This is the time to Hallelujah. Jesus, our king.

Part Two: "O" and "S"

Characters: All Chefs

Props: A long table or two short tables, seven plates, seven aprons, seven chef's hats, and seven pairs of gloves.

Yellow Yvonne: Our third ingredient for our humility sandwich begins with the letter "O." The ingredient is "obedient." "And being found in fashion as a man, He humbled Himself, and became obedient unto death, even the death of the cross" (Philippians 2:8). Jesus obeyed His Father, even in death. He wants us to be obedient in all that we do.

Chief Chef: Fellow chefs, place the "O" on the humility sandwich. (Everyone takes their "O," lifts it high in the air, and places it on each person's plate.)

Red Ralph: I am so glad that I did not hear the word "blood." I do a little praise dance every time I hear that word. (Excited) I cannot help myself. I need room to dance.

Green Gus: Our fourth ingredient for the humility sandwich begins with the letter "S." The ingredient is "sacrifice." "And almost all things are by the law purged with blood" (Hebrews 9:22a).

Red Ralph: (Excited) Did you say "blood"? I need to dance. (Red Ralph dances around the table.)

Green Gus: "And without shedding of (spell the word B-L-O-O-D) is no remission" (Hebrews 9:22b). Every time I hear the word sacrifice, I hear a melody of grace.

Chief Chef: Fellow chefs, place "S" on the humility sandwich. That word is in my heart again. Here is a song to feed our minds about sacrifice.

(Everyone takes their "S," lifts it high in the air, and places it on each person's plate.)

♫ *My Hands Are Out* ♫

My hands are out. My heart is pure.
I came to serve forever more.
No right or left. No left or right.
My eyes will be open tonight. (Repeat twice)

Part Two
Hallelujah, Hallelujah, Hallelujah, Hallelujah
Hallelujah, Hallelujah, Hallelujah, Hallelujah
The Lord's Prayer

Part Three: "E" and "N"

Characters: All Chefs

Props: A long table or two short tables, seven plates, seven aprons, seven chef's hats, and seven pairs of gloves.

Blue Betty: Our fifth ingredient for our humility sandwich begins with the letter "E." The ingredient is "exalt." "Wherefore, God also hath exalted Him, and given Him a name which is above every name" (Philippians 2:9). Exalt means to place in the highest honor.

Chief Chef: Fellow chefs, place "E" on the humility sandwich. (Everyone takes their "E," lifts it high in the air, and places it on each person's plate.)

Chief Chef: As we prepare to finish our humility sandwich (Pause), we take this time to gather our thoughts to allow our minds to be renewed by the word. (Pause) Think about the blood!

Red Ralph: (Excited) Did you say blood? I am ready to dance! (Red Ralph dances!)

Purple Paul: The sixth ingredient for our humility sandwich begins with the letter "N." The ingredient is "name." "That at the name of Jesus, every knee should bow, of things in heaven, and things in earth, and things under the earth: And that every tongue should confess that Jesus Christ is Lord, to the glory of God the Father" (Philippians 2:10-11).

Purple Paul: I think of the names of Jesus, such as Friend, Son of God, Savior, Good Shepherd, The Door, Bright Morning Star, Bread of Life, Living Water, Lamb of God, King of kings, Lion of the Tribe of Judah, and the True Vine.

Chief Chef: Fellow chefs, place "N" on the humility sandwich. (Everyone takes their "N," lifts it high in the air, and places it on each person's plate.)

♫ *At The Name of Jesus*♫

Isaiah 45:23-24, Philippians 2:5-11

At the name of Jesus, every knee shall bow.
At the name of Jesus, every knee shall bow.
At His name, the enemy trembles.
At His name, sick bodies are healed.
At the name of Jesus, every knee shall bow. Every knee shall bow.

The name of Jesus is holy and precious.
He's more than precious to me.
He is so great, the Son of the Highest.
He rules and reigns as our King.
His name is above every name. All things are under His feet. Come bow your
knees and worship Him.
Worship the Holy King at His name.

At the name of Jesus, every knee shall bow.
At the name of Jesus, every knee shall bow.
At His name, the enemy trembles
At His name, sick bodies are healed.
At the name of Jesus, every knee shall bow. Every knee shall bow.

At I'm gonna call on Jesus. At I'm gonna call on Jesus.
At I'm gonna call on Jesus. At I'm gonna call on Jesus.

At I said the enemy trembles. At I said the enemy trembles.
At I said the enemy trembles. At I said the enemy trembles.

At Jesus, Jesus, Jesus. At Jesus, Jesus, Jesus.
At Jesus, Jesus, Jesus. At Jesus, Jesus, Jesus. At the name of Jesus
Every knee shall bow. Every knee shall bow. Every knee shall bow.

Part Four: The Humility Agreement

Characters: All Chefs

Props: A long table or two short tables, seven plates, seven aprons, seven chef's hats, and seven pairs of gloves.

Chief Chef: When we mix the ingredients, the final product is "CHOSEN." The sandwich is complete. Let's review our ingredients from Philippians 2:5-11 and Hebrews 9:22.

Red Ralph: Our first ingredient is "Christ Jesus."

Orange Orin: Our second ingredient is "Himself."

Yellow Yvonne: Our third ingredient is "Obedient."

Green Gus: Our fourth ingredient is "Sacrifice."

Blue Betty: Our fifth ingredient is "Exalt."

Purple Paul: Our sixth ingredient is "Name."

Chief Chef: Fellow chefs, top this sandwich with love. You are ready to receive your badge from *The Making of the Humility Sandwich*. Raise your right hand and repeat after me. (Reading) The making of the humility sandwich

All Chefs: The making of the humility sandwich

Chief Chef: requires that I work together with my fellow chefs.

All Chefs: requires that I work together with my fellow chefs.

Chief Chef: I will share the humility of Jesus Christ daily.

All Chefs: I will share the humility of Jesus Christ daily.

Chief Chef: I will be humble in all things that I do.

All Chefs: I will be humble in all things that I do.

Chief Chef: I will finish my work with love. I will celebrate Jesus.

All Chefs: I will finish my work with love. I will celebrate Jesus.

Chief Chef: Amen!

All Chefs: Amen!

Chief Chef: Enjoy your meal! (pause) I have one more thing to say. (pause) Blood!

(Red Ralph dances.)

♫*Kingdom Kids*♫

Ephesians 4:7-11

We are kingdom kids, and we're here today to celebrate to celebrate.
We are kingdom kids, and we're here today to celebrate to celebrate.
The measure of the gift. The gift of Jesus. Grace He gave to us.
I have a measure. I will use my gift in the body of Christ. I will serve
the Lord all my life. (Repeat one time)

I will use it to perfect the Saints. I will use it for the ministry.
I will edify the body. I will give the Lord all of me. (Repeat once)
We are kingdom kids, and we're here today to celebrate.

The End

Book 5

When God Calls

Visual Experience of When God Calls

When God Calls is a major production that focuses on the covenant relationships that God established through Adam (Adamic Covenant), Abraham (Abrahamic Covenant), Noah (Noahic Covenant), Moses (Mosaic Covenant), Davidic (Davidic Covenant), and Jesus Christ (New Covenant).

A covenant is an agreement or promise between God and another person or group of people, often sealed with blood, to reach a common goal. Some covenants say that God will do something if someone does something (conditional). Some covenants say that God does something just because He is God and desires to show His love toward us (unconditional).

The main feature of each chapter expounds upon what each person did, faced, or left when they encountered God for the first time or heard the voice of God for the first time. Each chapter uncovers the covenant or promise as God established a relationship with a specific person.

God formed Adam from the dust of the ground. Noah built an ark. Abraham left his family. Moses delivered the children of Israel from bondage. David was anointed as king over Israel. Jesus Christ is the Savior of the world.

Sin created a barrier between God and man. Jesus Christ restored our relationship between God and man, but man must agree to the covenant's provisions. God desires a covenant relationship with us through His Son.

God also called all of us for a purpose. We can fulfill our purpose in life when we listen to God. This play includes children and adults. Prepare for a time of worship and praise. Your worship experience may grow after the teachings and performances. Praise the Lord!

Part One: Creation-The Edenic Covenant

Characters: Narrator, black and white costume, cloud, sea, tree, sun, moon, star, fish, bird, rabbit, a man, and a woman

Props: table, sheet, fruit, light, tools, and soil

Narrator: The scene opens with God speaking the world into existence. The first covenant of this play is the Edenic covenant. Genesis 1:28-29 provides the details of the Edenic covenant. The man and woman were responsible for having children, dominating and caring for the earth, and obeying God by abstaining from the forbidden fruit.

Narrator: "In the beginning, God created the heaven and the earth. And the earth was without form and void, and darkness was upon the face of the deep. And the Spirit of God moved upon the face of the waters" (Genesis 1:1-2).

Voice of God: On the first day, I speak day and night into being, and it is so (Genesis 1:3-5).

(The child enters wearing a black and white costume).

Voice of God: On the second day, I speak the sky into being, and it is so (Genesis 1:6-8). (Child enters as a cloud).

Voice of God: On the third day, I speak the dry land, seas, plants, and flowers into being, and it is so (Genesis 1:9-12).
(The child enters as a tree).

Voice of God: On the fourth day, I speak the sun, moon, and stars into being, and it is so (Genesis 1:14-19). (Three children enter as the sun, moon, and star).

Voice of God: On the fifth day, I speak the animals of the sea and the birds of the air into being, and it is so (Genesis 1:20-23). (Two children enter as a fish and a bird).

Voice of God: On the sixth day, I speak animals into being, and it is so (Genesis 1:24-25). (A child enters as a rabbit).

Voice of God: On the sixth day, let us make man in our own image (Genesis 1:26). (Adam enters.)

Narrator: God created man in His image, male and female. God said that everything that He made was good. He rested on the seventh day. "And the Lord God formed man of the dust of the ground, and breathed into his nostrils the breath of life, and man became a living soul" (Genesis 2:7). Adam lived in the Garden of Eden. He had dominion over it. God gave rules to Adam to follow.

Voice of God: "Of every tree of the garden thou mayest freely eat: but of the tree of the knowledge of good and evil, thou shalt not eat of it: for in the day that thou eatest thereof thou shalt surely die" (Genesis 2:16,17).

Narrator: God said it is not good for man to be alone. God took a rib from Adam when Adam slept and made a woman. It's amazing what God did. (The man and woman are visible during the song).

♫ *Sing a song about creation* ♫

It's Amazing
Genesis 1 and 2

God made the moon. He made the sun. He made the antelope to run.
A blade of grass can hold the dew. He made the earth for me and you.
But most of all, the amazing of all, it's amazing that my God made me. (Repeat)

It's amazing to me how my God so big can make someone so small like me.
It's amazing! It's amazing to me how my God so big can make someone so small
like me. It's amazing to me!

The sky is blue. The grass is green. There are wonders that we have never seen,
but they can't compare to the time when God made me. (Repeat)

It's amazing to me how my God so big can make someone so small like me.
It's amazing, oh yes, it is! It's amazing to me how my God so big can make
someone so small like me. It's amazing, oh yes, it is!

It's amazing! It's amazing! It's amazing! It's amazing! To me. To me.

End of Part One.

Part Two: The Fall of Man-The Adamic Covenant

Characters: Narrator, Voice of God, Adam, Eve,

Props: area of the garden

Narrator: The fall of man began when a crafty serpent approached the woman about the forbidden tree one day. A conversation occurred between the serpent and the woman. They debated God's Word. Before long, the woman ate from the forbidden tree, and so did her husband. Their actions of sin broke the Edenic covenant with God. (They hide from God). They experience the Adamic covenant, found in Genesis 3:15, which details the serpent's curse, the redemptive work of Christ on the cross, and the sorrow of humanity.

Voice of God: Serpent, you are cursed above all beasts. You will move on your belly. You will eat dust every day of your life. (Gen. 3:14) (pause) "I will put enmity between thee and the woman, and between thy seed and her seed; it shall bruise thy head, and thou shalt bruise His heel" (Genesis 3:15). (pause) Woman, in life, I will multiply your sorrow. You will bring forth children, you will desire your husband, and he shall rule over you (Genesis 3:16). (pause) Man, you will not eat of the tree. The ground has a curse. In sorrow, you will eat of the ground containing thistles. You will return to the ground.

(Genesis 3: 17-19). (With emphasis) Leave the garden.

(Adam and Eve leave the Garden of Eden with their heads hanging low.)

Narrator: The punishment for sin is death. Corruption continued upon the earth until the Bible introduced Noah.
End of Part Two

Part Three: The Rainbow-The Noahic Covenant

Characters: Voice of God, Narrator, Noah, Noah's Wife, Shem, Shem's Wife, Japheth, Japheth's Wife, six children dressed as animals (two of the same kind), and three mockers

Props: rainbow, an ark with a door, tools, a light, animals, and sound effects of rain.

(The scene opens with the ark in the center of the stage.)

Narrator: Adam sinned. God knows that we are not perfect. He loves us even when we do wrong. He has a purpose for our lives even when we mess up. He gives us grace. God thought to destroy man due to sin with a flood. "But Noah found grace in the eyes of the Lord" (Genesis 6:8). Noah built an ark to save his family from the flood. The flood destroyed everyone except Noah and his family and the animals. Sin was in the land, and sin does not please God.

Voice of God: "My spirit shall not always strive with man for that he is also flesh, yet his days shall be a hundred and twenty years" (Genesis 6:3).

Narrator: "God saw that wickedness was great in the earth" (Genesis 6:5a), "and it grieved Him at His heart" (Genesis 6:b).

(Noah walks in)

Narrator: "But Noah found grace in the eyes of the Lord" (Genesis 6:8).

(He kneels before the Lord at center stage).

Voice of God: "Noah, the end of all flesh has come before me" (Genesis 6:13a); sin is in the heart of man. Make an ark of gopher wood and follow my instructions. Bring your family and animals into the ark as I instruct you. I will destroy all flesh. "I will establish my covenant with you" (Genesis 6:18a).

Noah: Yes, Lord! (Genesis 6:22).

Narrator: I am sure that people wondered about the ark. What was an ark? What was its purpose? Why did they have animals in it? In my imagination, people made fun of Noah and his family, but Noah followed God in every detail.

(Noah's family enters and all pretend to build the ark).

(Two sets of the same animals enter the ark.)

Noah: I do all that the Lord commands.

(Another set of the same animals enter the ark).

Noah: I do all that the Lord commands.

(The last set of animals enter the ark.)

Noah: I do all that the Lord commands.

(The sound effects of rain begin.)

Voice of God: I will shut you in (Genesis 6:16b).

Narrator: It rained for forty days and forty nights. All flesh died except Noah, his family, and the animals on the ark (Genesis 612, 14-16). After many days, Noah, his family, and the animals left the ark.

(They leave the ark.)

(Noah kneels before the Lord and sacrifices an animal to the Lord).

Voice of God: "Noah and sons, be fruitful, and multiply, and replenish the earth" (Genesis 9:1). "This is the token of the covenant which I make between me and you and every living creature that is with you, for perpetual generations" (Genesis: 9:12). When you see a rainbow in the clouds, it is my promise, my covenant that I will not destroy the earth with a flood again (Genesis 9:15).

♫ *Sing a song about being aware of God's presence* ♫

Open Our Eyes

Open our eyes to the things before us. Open our eyes to the ways that you move. Open our eyes so that we do not miss you for you are speaking a word in us. (Repeat)

Come into the service. Touch this one and that. Move all through the pews from the front to the back. Anoint us and make us a sight to behold. Open our eyes, Lord. (Repeat)

Open our eyes. Open our eyes. Open our eyes. Open our eyes.
Open our eyes, open our eyes, open our eyes. Open our eyes.
Open our eyes, open our eyes, open our eyes. Open our eyes.

Psalm 119:18 says, Open thou mine eyes, that I behold wondrous things out of thy law.

Open our eyes. Open our eyes. Open my eyes, Father. End of Part Three

Part Four: The Abrahamic Covenant

Characters: Narrator, Voice of God, Abraham, Sarah, Lot, and Melchizedek

Props: An altar, Tithes, offerings, bread, drink, and gifts

(The scene opens with Abram looking at his land.)

Narrator: Sin repeated itself after the time of Noah. Abram was a descendent of Noah. God called Abram, later changed to Abraham, out of the country of Ur and his father's house to an unknown land. Abraham followed God by faith. God blessed Abraham with an unconditional promise through the Abrahamic Covenant.

(Abram tends to the sheep in the middle of the stage. He looks up when God calls him.)

Voice of God: Abram, get out of Ur, leave your father, and go to a place that I choose. I will bless your nation; I will bless you. I will bless your name. You will be a blessing. I will bless them that bless you and curse them that curse you. Blessings come through you to other families (Genesis 12:1-3).

Abram: Sarai, Lot, we must leave our home and go to a land of God's choice. Gather the animals, our substance, and souls and leave our home.

Sarai: Abram, did God tell you where to go?

Lot: Did He tell you to travel north, south, east, or west?

Abram: God told me to leave my father's house at 75 years old, and He would show me where to go (Genesis 12:4).

Voice of God: Abram, I will give this land unto your seed (Genesis 12:7).

(Abram built an altar, and he worshiped the Lord.)

Abram: Lord, I worship you, I praise you. You are worthy of being praised in the land of your choice. (Kneels before the Lord)

Narrator: Due to differences of opinion, Abram and Lot separated. Abram continued his journey with Sarai. Do you think that Abram questioned God? I am sure Abram wondered about God's promises because he had no children and was 75, but God renewed His promise to Abram.

Voice of God: Abram, look up to the north, south, east, and west. (Abram looks) I will make your seed as the dust of the earth. Walk through the land. (Abram walks left and right) Everything is yours! (Genesis 13:14-17). (Abram stays in the middle of the stage.)

Narrator: Abram faced the battle of the kings. After the war, Melchizedek, king of Sodom, blessed Abram. Melchizedek was the priest of the most high God (Genesis 14:18).

(Melchizedek, with bread and drink, meets with Abram at the center of the stage. Abram kneels before him)

Melchizedek: "Blessed be Abram of the high God, possessor of heaven and earth: and blessed be the most high God, who allowed you to win the battle" (Genesis 14:19-20). (He gives drink and bread to Abram. Abram gives tithes and offerings to Melchizedek.)

Voice of God: "Fear not, Abram: I am thy shield and thy exceeding great reward" (Genesis 15:1)

Abram: Lord God, I do not have a child (Genesis 15:2).

Voice of God: The seed shall come from your own bowels (Genesis 15:4). Your seed shall look like the number of the stars (Genesis 15:5).

Abram: (lifting his hands) I believe you, God!

Narrator: "And he believed in the Lord, and he counted it to him for righteousness" (Genesis 15:6).

Narrator: God spoke to Abram again when he turned 99 years old. God told him to walk before him and be perfect. God emphasized the blessing of his seed and the promise of land. God changed his name to Abraham. God told Abraham that circumcision signified a token of the covenant between them. God changed Sarai to Sarah. He blessed them with a child named Isaac (Genesis 17:1-19). Sin continued in the land.

Step of Faith

2 Corinthians 5:7 and Philippians 3:14

I'm taking a step of faith. I'm walking with the Lord.
I can't see my way around. I'll put one foot on the ground.
I press toward the mark above. It's full steam ahead.
I'm on my way. I'm moving ahead. I'm moving ahead.

I'm taking a step, a step of faith.
The power of God is my life. I'm moving ahead.
I'm taking a step, a step of faith.
The power of God is my life. I'm moving ahead.

I'm taking a step of faith. I'm walking with the Lord.
I can't see my way around. I'll put one foot on the ground.
I press toward the mark above. It's full steam ahead.
I'm on my way. I'm moving ahead. I'm moving ahead.

The power of God is my life. I'm moving ahead.
I'm taking a step, a step of faith.
The power of God is my life. I'm moving ahead.

Nothing can stop me. Nothing can block me.
I'm on my way now, a step of faith.
Nothing can stop me. Nothing can block me.
I'm on my way now.

The power of God is in my life. I'm moving ahead.
The power of God is in my life. I'm moving ahead.
The power of God is in my life. I'm moving ahead.

End of Part Four

Part Five: The Mosaic Covenant

Characters: Narrator, Voice of God, Moses, Four Levitical Priests, and a group of children as the children of Israel

Props: Burning bush, sandals, Ten Commandments, Ark of the Covenant, and a stick

(The burning bush is in the middle of the stage.)

Narrator: "Now Moses kept the flock of his father-in-law the priest of Midian: and he led the flock to the backside of the desert, and came to the mountain of God, even to Horeb. And the angel of the Lord appeared unto him in a flame of fire out of the midst of a bush: and he looked, and, behold, the bush burned with fire, and the bush was not consumed" (Exodus 3:1-2).

Moses: (He enters the stage with his stick in hand. He looks at the burning bush, then looks away.) "I will now turn aside and see this great sight, why the bush is not burnt" (Genesis 3:4).

Voice of God: "Moses, Moses" (Exodus 3:4c).

Moses: "Here I am" (Exodus 3:4d).

Voice of God: Take off your shoes for you are standing on Holy ground (Exodus 3:5). (Moses takes off his shoes.) I am the God of Abraham, Isaac, and Jacob. Go to Pharaoh and tell him that I want him to let my people go from his bondage. You will lead my people out of Egypt.
(Exodus 3:6-10).

Moses: Who am I that I should go to Pharoah? Who shall I say is sending me for such a task? (Exodus 3:11, 13).

Voice of God: "I AM THAT I AM" (Exodus 3:14a).

Moses: Lord, I don't talk very well. How can I go before anyone?

Voice of God: Aaron, your brother speaks well. You shall speak to Aaron and put words in his mouth: and I will be with your mouth and his mouth and teach you what you shall do (Exodus 4:14-15).

(The children of Israel join Moses. They walk around the stage. The Levitical priests carry the Ark of the Covenant on poles. Moses separates from the children of Israel.)

Narrator: Even after escaping Egypt, they experience the ten plagues, follow the Ark of the Covenant, cross the Red Sea, cross the Jordan River, receive manna, and see the water from the rock. The Israelites continue to forget the blessings of God.

Moses: I will go to Mt. Sinai to hear from the Lord. (Moses leaves the stage and then returns with the Ten Commandments.) Elders and Israelites, I have the Word from the Lord for you to receive. (Holding up the Ten Commandments) We must abide by all that the Lord says.

Narrator: God introduced the Mosaic Covenant in Exodus 19:5-8. The covenant contained commandments, social requirements, and ordinances to reveal sin. This covenant did not save people, nor did it stop sin, but it led people to a perfect Savior, the promised seed, the One, coming through the line of David. "For the law was given by Moses, but grace and truth came by Jesus Christ: (John 1:17). Sin continued in the land.

♫ *In The Beginning* ♫

John 1:1-14, Psalm 119:105.

In the beginning, was the Word. And the Word was with God, and the Word was God. The word began with God. The word started with God. (Repeat)

I said the word; the word will light my day.
I said the word; the word will make a way.
I said the word; the word will save my soul.
I said the word; the word will make me whole.

In the beginning, was the Word.
And the Word was with God, and the Word was God.
The word began with God. The word began with God.

I said the word; the word will light my day.
I said the word; the word will make a way.
I said the word; the word will save my soul.
I said the word; the word will make me whole.

Thy word is a lamp unto my feet; thy word is a light unto my path.
Thy word is a lamp unto my feet; thy word is a light unto my path.
Thy word is a lamp unto my feet; thy word is a light unto my path.
Thy word is a lamp unto my feet, thy word thy word, thy word.

I said the word; the word will light my day.
I said the word; the word will make a way.
I said the word; the word will save my soul.
I said the word; the word will make me whole.

In the beginning, was the Word.
And the Word was with God, and the Word was God.
The word began with God. The word began with God.
End Part Five.

Part Six: Davidic Covenant

Characters: Voice of God, Narrator, David, Nathan, Jesse, Samuel, Four Levitical Priests, and seven sons of Jesse

Props: Holy of Holies, Ark of the Covenant, a chair, and a rag, anointing oil

(The scene opens with Samuel the Prophet standing at center stage.)

Narrator: David was a shepherd who cared for sheep. God called David, at a young age, as the king of Israel. Samuel the Prophet anointed David for his calling as king among his father and brothers. Although he did not become king until several years later, David obeyed God's call. David loved to praise the Lord. When David sinned, he asked for forgiveness and still praised the Lord. God established His kingdom through the line of David for His kingdom to last forever.

(Samuel enters the stage. He looks very sad.)

Voice of God: "How long will you mourn for Saul, seeing I have rejected him from reigning over Israel? Fill thy horn with oil, and go, I send you to Jesse the Bethlehemite: for I have provided me a king among his sons" (1 Samuel 16:1).

Samuel: Saul will not like this of me (1 Samuel 16:2).

Voice of God: Samuel, go, and sacrifice to the Lord (1 Samuel 16:2).

(Samuel leaves. Jesse enters and cleans around the stage)

(Samuel knocks, and Jesse answers the door. They talk)

Jesse: Samuel, do you come in peace? 1 Samuel 16:4)

Samuel: I come to you in peace. The Lord sent me here today to anoint the next king of Israel among one of your sons (1 Samuel 16:4-5).

Jesse: Look at my first son, Eliab. (Eliab walks to Samuel.) 1 Samuel 16:6)

Samuel: Surely, the Lord's anointed is before me. (1 Samuel 16:6).

Voice of God: "Look not on his countenance or on the height of his stature, because I refused him: for the Lord sees not as man sees; for man looks at the outward appearance, but the Lord looks at the heart" (1 Samuel 16:7).

(The other sons pass before Samuel, but he does not show approval.)

Samuel: (Looking to Jesse) Do you have any other children? (1 Samuel 16:11b)

Jesse: There is the youngest. He is with the sheep (1 Samuel 16:11c).

Samuel: Go get him! (1 Samuel 16:11d).

(Jesse leaves and returns with David.)

Voice of God: "Arise, anoint him: for this is he" (1 Samuel 16:13).

(Samuel anoints David among his father and brothers. Everyone exits.)

Narrator: Several years passed before the first anointing as king and David's arrival on the throne as king. David missed the Ark of the Covenant. The Ark represented the presence of God. David brought the Ark home with a grand celebration. David recovered the Ark of the Covenant at Kirjath-jearim at the home of Obed-edom. (2 Samuel 6). The four Levitical priests carry the Ark of the Covenant on four poles. David dances before the Ark with great power and strength.

(Add supportive music for the celebration. After they dance, they place the Ark into the Holy of Holies).

(Nathan enters the stage with David. David kneels before him.)

Voice of God: Nathan, I will give you my word for you to speak to my servant, David. (2 Samuel 7:4-5).

Narrator: The Lord speaks the Davidic Covenant, the unconditional promise of God, through Nathan to David. It explains the rulership of Jesus Christ through the line of David.

Nathan: "The Lord of hosts says, I took thee from the sheepcote, from following the sheep, to be ruler over my people Israel. The Lord will plant his people. He will make a house. And when your days be fulfilled, and you shall sleep with your fathers, He will set up His seed after you, which shall come out of your bowels. He will establish His kingdom. He will establish his throne forever" (2 Samuel 8-17.)

My Hands Are Out

Psalm 90:17

My hands are out. My heart is pure. I came to serve forever more.
No right or left. No left or right. My eyes will be open tonight.
(Repeat two times)

Hallelujah. Hallelujah. Hallelujah. Hallelujah.
Hallelujah. Hallelujah. Hallelujah. Hallelujah.

The Lord's prayer

End of Part Six

Part Seven: New Covenant

Characters: Narrator, John the Baptist, Jesus, The Crowd, Holy Spirit
(Dove), a Sick Person, a Blind Person, Mother of Jesus, Simon,
Disciples, Centurion, and Angels

Props: Ark of the Covenant, Garden of Gethsemane, Holy of
Holies, Crown of Thorns, Scarlet Robe, and Cross

Narrator: Man needed a Savior because of sin. "For all have sinned,
and come short of the glory of God" (Romans 3:23). A perfect
sacrifice was the only way to save humankind from eternal death.
Who was God going to call next? "And there shall come forth a rod
out of the stem of Jesse, and a Branch shall grow out of his roots"
(Isaiah 11:1). Jesus Christ, the perfect redeemer, was next. He came
to save people from sin.

(John the Baptist enters.)

John the Baptist: "The voice of one crying in the wilderness,
prepare ye the way of the Lord, make His paths straight" (Mark 1:3).
Repent, repent, repent! "There cometh one mightier than I after me,
the latchet of whose shoes I am not worthy to stoop down and
unloose" (Mark 1:7).

(Look at Jesus; John the Baptist baptizes Jesus.)

Holy Spirit: (A child holding a dove or dressed as a dove comes
along the side of Jesus).

Voice of God: "Thou art my beloved Son, in whom I am well
pleased" (Mark 1:11b).

(Jesus leaves.)

Narrator: John the Baptist knew Jesus as the Lamb of God after the Holy Spirit descended from heaven and remained with Jesus. (John 1:31-34). After the baptism, Satan tempted Jesus in the wilderness for 40 days, and the angels ministered to Him. Jesus began preaching the gospel of the kingdom of God.

(Jesus enters with a crowd. Hands out.)

Jesus: "The time is fulfilled, and the kingdom of God is at hand: repent ye, and believe the gospel" (Mark 1:15). Follow me: Simon Peter, James, John, Andrew, Philip, Bartholomew, Matthew, Thomas, James, Thaddeus, Simon, and Judas.

(Twelve men follow Jesus as He moves to a high place in the church.)

Sick Person: (Walking by Jesus) I am healed. Thank you, Jesus!

Blind Person: (Walking by Jesus) I can see. Thank you, Jesus!

Jesus: (With great emphasis) "Behold, we go up to Jerusalem; and the Son of man shall be delivered unto the chief priests, and unto the scribes; and they shall condemn Him to death, and shall deliver Him to the Gentiles: And they shall mock Him, and shall scourge Him, and shall spit upon Him, and shall kill Him: and the third day He shall rise again" (Mark 10:33-34).

Narrator: James and John desired to sit on the right and left of Jesus in glory, but Jesus reminded them that the most incredible place to be is in a position of servanthood. In later days, those in Jerusalem experienced Jesus' grand entrance into the area on a donkey, which fulfilled Old Testament prophecy. Later in his ministry, Jesus said that one of His disciples would betray Him. This scene continues in the Garden of Gethsemane. The disciples fall asleep as Jesus talks with the Father.

Jesus: Sit while I pray (Mark 14:32c). Tarry and watch (Mark 14:34b)

(One by one, the disciples fall asleep.)

Jesus: (Praying) Abba, Father, all things are possible unto thee; take away this cup from me; nevertheless, not my will but your will (Mark 14:36)

(Jesus sees the disciples sleeping, and everyone wakes up.)

Jesus: Simon, could you watch but one hour? Watch and pray. The spirit is ready, but the flesh is weak (Mark 14:37-38). (They fall asleep).

Jesus: (Praying) Abba, Father, all things are possible unto thee; take away this cup from me; nevertheless, not my will but your will (Mark 14:39)

Jesus: You are sleeping again (Mark 14:40). (Praying) Abba, Father, all things are possible unto thee; take away this cup from me; nevertheless, not my will but your will (Mark 14:41)

Jesus: Rise up. (Everyone gets up.) My time of betrayal is here (Mark 14:42).

Narrator: Many betrayed Jesus, especially Judas Iscariot. Chief people presented Jesus before the high priest. One disciple, Simon Peter, denied Jesus three times. Elders, along with the whole council, gave Jesus before Pilate. The crowd shouted to release Barrabas, a robber, and crucify Jesus, an innocent man. Pilate listened to the crowd.

The Crowd: Crucify Him! Crucify Him! Crucify Him! (Mark 15:13).

(Jesus enters on a cross. He wears a crown of thorns and a scarlet robe.
The people watch Him as He hangs on the cross.)

Mother of Jesus: (She watches as Jesus hangs on the cross.)

Jesus: "My God, My God, why hast thou forsaken me?" (Mark 15:34c)

(Someone lifts a sponge filled with vinegar to Jesus' mouth.) Mark 15:36

Jesus: "It is finished" (Mark 15:37)

Centurion: "Truly this man was the Son of God" (Mark 15:39c).

(They carry Jesus away.)

Narrator: Jesus died for the sins of the world. He fulfilled the elements of a perfect sacrifice for humankind's sins, but how will He rise after His death? When many of His friends and family arrived at the tomb, Jesus' body was not there. Where did He go?

(As soft music plays, the angels escort all cast members down the aisle to the altar. Jesus appears behind the Holy of Holies when all kneel at the altar. Everyone rejoices!

Narrator: "Behold, the days come, saith the Lord, that I will make a new covenant with the house of Israel, and with the house of Judah" (Jeremiah 31:31). Jesus Christ solidified the future of the New Covenant by living, dying, rising, and ascending back to heaven according to the Scriptures. The Lord opened the gift of grace to all who believe in the sacrificial work of Jesus Christ by faith. Jesus

Christ fulfills the call for the Edenic, Adamic, Noahic, Abrahamic, Mosaic, Davidic, and New Covenants upon the experience of eternal life. Jesus Christ answered and lived the call when God called for the future of humankind. Amen.

97

♫ *The Way* ♫

John 14:6

He is the way, the truth, the life, the way. (Repeat seven times)

"Let not your heart be troubled: ye believe in God, believe also in me. In my Father's house are many mansions: if it were not so, I would have told you. I go to prepare a place for you. And if I go and prepare a place for you, I will come again, and receive you unto myself; that where I am, there ye may be also. And whither I go ye know, and the way ye know. Thomas saith unto him, Lord, we know not whither thou goest; and how can we know the way? Jesus saith unto him, I am the way, the truth, and the life: no man cometh unto the Father, but by me."

The End

Book 6

Music in the Air: A Christmas Musical

Visual Experience of Music in the Air:
A Christmas Musical

The visual experience of *Music in the Air: A Christmas Musical* expresses the reading of the traditional Scriptures relating to the birth of Jesus Christ from St. Luke Chapters One and Two accompanied by original modern Scripture-based musical selections.

The musical's setting encapsulates the season's beauty with bold red, green, silver, and gold colors. The attire reflects boys in classy suits and ties and girls in dresses with fancy hair. The creative mindset of the scenery represents holiness.

The emotion of the musical creates a liveliness of what it may have been like to see an angel tell a young virgin that she was to give birth to the Savior of the world or that her soul magnifies the God that lives in her. What a blessing to write this musical!

The musical has four sets of Scriptures and four songs. The musical gets to the point very quickly. An excellent reader reads the Scriptures, and the children follow with a joyous song. This works for those on a limited schedule who want a quality message. Enjoy!

Part One: Nothing is Impossible

St. Luke 1:26-38

[26] "And in the sixth month the angel Gabriel was sent from God unto a city of Galilee, named Nazareth,

[27] To a virgin espoused to a man whose name was Joseph, of the house of David; and the virgin's name was Mary.

[28] And the angel came in unto her, and said, Hail, thou that art highly favoured, the Lord is with thee: blessed art thou among women.

[29] And when she saw him, she was troubled at his saying, and cast in her mind what manner of salutation this should be.

[30] And the angel said unto her, Fear not, Mary: for thou hast found favour with God.

[31] And, behold, thou shalt conceive in thy womb, and bring forth a son, and shalt call his name JESUS.

[32] He shall be great, and shall be called the Son of the Highest: and the Lord God shall give unto him the throne of his father David:

[33] And he shall reign over the house of Jacob for ever; and of his kingdom there shall be no end.

[34] Then said Mary unto the angel, How shall this be, seeing I know not a man?

[35] And the angel answered and said unto her, The Holy Ghost shall come upon thee, and the power of the Highest shall overshadow thee: therefore also that holy thing which shall be born of thee shall be called the Son of God.

[36] And, behold, thy cousin Elisabeth, she hath also conceived a son in her old age: and this is the sixth month with her, who was called barren.

[37] For with God nothing shall be impossible.

[38] And Mary said, Behold the handmaid of the Lord; be it unto me according to thy word. And the angel departed from her" (St. Luke 1:26-38).

♫*Nothing is Impossible*♫

St. Luke 1:34-37

With God, dear child, nothing is impossible.
With God, dear child, nothing is impossible.
The Holy Ghost shall come upon thee, and the power of the Highest
shall overshadow thee. Just believe me. That Holy One in thee shall
be called the Son of God, the Son of God, the Son of God.

With God, dear child, nothing is impossible. With God, dear child,
nothing is impossible.

Part Two: My Soul Doth Magnify the Lord

St. Luke 1:39-56

[39] "And Mary arose in those days, and went into the hill country with haste, into a city of Juda;

[40] And entered into the house of Zacharias, and saluted Elisabeth.

[41] And it came to pass, that, when Elisabeth heard the salutation of Mary, the babe leaped in her womb; and Elisabeth was filled with the Holy Ghost:

[42] And she spake out with a loud voice, and said, Blessed art thou among women, and blessed is the fruit of thy womb.

[43] And whence is this to me, that the mother of my Lord should come to me?

[44] For, lo, as soon as the voice of thy salutation sounded in mine ears, the babe leaped in my womb for joy.

[45] And blessed is she that believed: for there shall be a performance of those things which were told her from the Lord.

[46] And Mary said, My soul doth magnify the Lord,

[47] And my spirit hath rejoiced in God my Saviour.

[48] For he hath regarded the low estate of his handmaiden: for, behold, from henceforth all generations shall call me blessed.

[49] For he that is mighty hath done to me great things; and holy is his name.

[50] And his mercy is on them that fear him from generation to generation.

[51] He hath shewed strength with his arm; he hath scattered the proud in the imagination of their hearts.

[52] He hath put down the mighty from their seats, and exalted them of low degree.

[53] He hath filled the hungry with good things; and the rich he hath sent empty away.

[54] He hath helped his servant Israel, in remembrance of his mercy;

[55] As he spake to our fathers, to Abraham, and to his seed for ever.

[56] And Mary abode with her about three months, and returned to her own house" (St. Like 39-56).

♫ *My Soul Doth Magnify the Lord* ♫

St. Luke 1:46-56

My soul doth magnify the Lord, and my spirit hath rejoiced in God my Savior.
He knows that I am low, but I am blessed and holy is His name.

My soul doth magnify the Lord, and my spirit hath rejoiced in God my Savior.
He knows that I am low, but I am blessed and holy is His name.

He is mighty. Mighty is His name. He has done great, great things for me.
And His mercy is on them that fear Him. Holy, holy is His name. Holy, holy is
His name.

I'm the seed of Abraham. Holy is His name.
I'm the seed of Abraham. Holy is His name.
From generation to generation, holy, holy is His name.
From generation to generation, holy, holy is His name.

Holy, Holy is His name.
Holy, Holy is His name.

Part Three: This is the Time to Celebrate

St. Luke 2:1-7

[1] "And it came to pass in those days, that there went out a decree from Caesar Augustus that all the world should be taxed.
[2] (And this taxing was first made when Cyrenius was governor of Syria.)
[3] And all went to be taxed, every one into his own city.
[4] And Joseph also went up from Galilee, out of the city of Nazareth, into Judaea, unto the city of David, which is called Bethlehem; (because he was of the house and lineage of David:)
[5] To be taxed with Mary his espoused wife, being great with child.
[6] And so it was, that, while they were there, the days were accomplished that she should be delivered.
[7] And she brought forth her firstborn son, and wrapped him in swaddling clothes, and laid him in a manger; because there was no room for them in the inn" (St. Luke 2:1-9).

♫*This is the Time to Celebrate*♫

Part One
This is the time to celebrate.
This is the time to celebrate.
This is the time to celebrate Jesus, our king.

Part Two
We're going to adore for He's wonderful and He is the mighty God.
Bow down before Him as the king of kings. I will give Him my all.
He's Alpha and Omega. He is the first, and He is the very last.
He is my Savior. He is my friend. He has washed me from my past.

Part Three
This is the time to Hallelujah.
This is the time to celebrate.
This is the time to Hallelujah. Jesus, our king.

Part Four: Music in the Air

St. Luke 2:8-14

[8] "And there were in the same country shepherds abiding in the field, keeping watch over their flock by night.
[9] And, lo, the angel of the Lord came upon them, and the glory of the Lord shone round about them: and they were sore afraid.
[10] And the angel said unto them, Fear not: for, behold, I bring you good tidings of great joy, which shall be to all people.
[11] For unto you is born this day in the city of David a Saviour, which is Christ the Lord.
[12] And this shall be a sign unto you; Ye shall find the babe wrapped in swaddling clothes, lying in a manger.
[13] And suddenly there was with the angel a multitude of the heavenly host praising God, and saying,
[14] Glory to God in the highest, and on earth peace, good will toward men" (St. Luke 2:8-14).

♫Music in the Air♫

When Jesus was born, there was music in the air.
The angel said fear not. Enjoy the music in the air.
Good tidings of great joy was the music in the air.
Glory in the highest became the music in the air.

I can hear music, music, music in the air.
I can hear angels, angels, angels everywhere.
There was a sign of the promise, a babe in swaddling clothes.
Lying in a manger then they saw the heavenly host.

For unto us a child is born, a Savior Christ the Lord.
For unto us a child is born, a Savior Christ the Lord.
For unto us a child is born, a Savior Christ the Lord.
For unto us a child is born, a Savior Christ the Lord.

For unto us a child is born a Savior Christ the Lord.
Music in the air.

The End

Book 7

Easter: This is the Time to Celebrate

The Visual Experience of Easter
This is the Time to Celebrate

The visual experience of *Easter, This is the Time to Celebrate Jesus, Our King,* depicts four stages of the purpose of Jesus' life for the salvation of humankind. This play dissects four scenes from other plays *When God Calls, Open Our Open Eyes, Three Miracles, and an Anointing,* to create an entirely new play for Easter.

Part One: Repent introduces the world to John the Baptist. He was the cousin and forerunner of Jesus Christ. John proclaimed repentance and the good news of the arrival of Jesus Christ. John baptized Jesus Christ in the Jordan River. The next day, he realized that Jesus was the Lamb of God who came to take away the sins of the world.

Part Two is a miracle occurring at a pool when Jesus healed a paralyzed man. The man obeyed the words of Jesus and received his healing when he followed Jesus' commands. Along with the miracles, a woman thought enough of Jesus to anoint His body for burial amid the presence of a selfish disciple.

Amid a group, Part Three shows how a woman poured perfume on Jesus' head. She wiped His feet with her hair. She sacrificed the most precious thing in her possession, the alabaster oil, while Jesus sacrificed the most precious thing He had, which was His life.

The death, burial, and resurrection of Jesus Christ, Part Four, unveils His sacrificial life for humankind as He prepares to fulfill some of the details of the New Covenant. Sin created a barrier between God and man. Jesus Christ restored our relationship between God and man, but man must agree to the covenant's provisions. God desires a covenant relationship with us through His Son. We celebrate when we accept Jesus Christ as our Savior.

Part One: Repent

Characters: Narrator, John the Baptist, Jesus, The Crowd, Holy Spirit (Dove), a Sick Person, a Blind Person, Mother of Jesus, Simon, Disciples, Centurion, and Angels

Props: Ark of the Covenant, Garden of Gethsemane, Holy of Holies, Crown of Thorns, Scarlet Robe, and Cross

Narrator: Man needed a Savior because of sin. "For all have sinned, and come short of the glory of God" (Romans 3:23). A perfect sacrifice was the only way to save humankind from eternal death. Who was God going to call next? "And there shall come forth a rod out of the stem of Jesse, and a Branch shall grow out of his roots" (Isaiah 11:1). Jesus Christ came as our Savior.

(John the Baptist enters.)

John the Baptist: "The voice of one crying in the wilderness, prepare ye the way of the Lord, make His paths straight" (Mark 1:3). Repent, repent, repent! "There cometh one mightier than I after me, the latchet of whose shoes I am not worthy to stoop down and unloose" (Mark 1:7).

(Look at Jesus; John the Baptist baptizes Jesus.)

Holy Spirit: (A child holding a dove or dressed as a dove comes along the side of Jesus).

Voice of God: "Thou art my beloved Son, in whom I am well pleased" (Mark 1:11b).

(John leaves.)

Jesus: "The time is fulfilled, and the kingdom of God is at hand: repent ye, and believe the gospel" (Mark 1:15). The Son of man came to open the eyes of those who are lost. The Son of man called twelve disciples cast out unclean spirits, healed a man with leprosy, and healed a paralyzed man. The Son of man ate with sinners, healed on the Sabbath, taught from parables, calmed the storm, raised a little girl from the dead, fed thousands of people, walked on water, healed a deaf and mute man, and healed a blind man. The Son of man came to open the eyes of the blind! The Son of man will be seen by many, suffer many things, be rejected by many, be killed, and after three days, rise again. Repent and believe the gospel!

(Everyone leaves.)

Narrator: The Bible says that John the Baptist did not know Jesus as the Lamb of God until after the baptism. The Holy Spirit descended from heaven like a dove and remained with Jesus. (John 1:31-34). After the baptism, Satan tempted Jesus in the wilderness for 40 days, and the angels ministered to Him. Jesus began preaching the gospel of the kingdom of God.

♫ *Repent and Be Baptized* ♫

I've come with a message today. A message of hope to live every day.
Open our open eyes. Repent and be baptized.
The message is simple. The message is right.
Repent and be baptized.

I've come with a message today. A message of hope to live every day.
Open our open eyes. Repent and be baptized.
The message is simple. The message is right.
Repent and be baptized.

I've come with a message today. A message of hope to live every day.
Open our open eyes. Repent and be baptized.
The message is simple. The message is right.
Repent and be baptized.

Open our open eyes
Repent and be baptized.
The message is simple. The message is right.
Repent and be baptized.

(Everyone leaves.)

End of Part One

Part Two: Jesus Heals the Paralyzed Man

John 5:1-9

Characters: Narrator, Jesus, a Man

Props: Bed, pool, and sound effects of water

Narrator: The book of John shares a miracle about how Jesus healed a paralyzed man at the pool of Bethesda. When an angel troubled the water, the first person in the water received a healing. The man, lying at the pool for 38 years, converses with Jesus about his condition. Jesus healed the man when the man obeyed the words of Jesus.

Jesus: (Walking to the man) Do you want to be whole? (John 5:6b)

Man: (Laying by the pool) I don't have anyone to put me into the water. When the troubling of the water occurs, someone steps in the water before me (John 4:7).

Jesus: Rise, take up your bed, and walk! (John 5:8)

Man: (The man gets up, takes his bed, and walks. (John 5:9).

♫ *Step of Faith* ♫

2 Corinthians 5:7 and Philippians 3:14

I'm taking a step of faith. I'm walking with the Lord.
I can't see my way around. I'll put one foot on the ground.
I press toward the mark above. It's full steam ahead.
I'm on my way. I'm moving ahead. I'm moving ahead.

I'm taking a step, a step of faith.
The power of God is my life. I'm moving ahead.
I'm taking a step, a step of faith.
The power of God is my life. I'm moving ahead.

I'm taking a step of faith. I'm walking with the Lord.
I can't see my way around. I'll put one foot on the ground.
I press toward the mark above. It's full steam ahead.
I'm on my way. I'm moving ahead. I'm moving ahead.

I'm taking a step, a step of faith.
The power of God is my life. I'm moving ahead.
I'm taking a step, a step of faith.
The power of God is my life. I'm moving ahead.
Nothing can stop me. Nothing can block me.

I'm on my way now, a step of faith.
Nothing can stop me. Nothing can block me.
I'm on my way now.

The power of God is in my life. I'm moving ahead.
The power of God is in my life. I'm moving ahead.
The power of God is in my life. I'm moving ahead.

End of Part Two

Part Three: A Woman Anoints Jesus

St. Matthew 26:6-13, St. Mark 14:1-11, St. Luke 7:36-50, St. John 12:1-8

Characters: Narrator, Jesus, Simon the leper, Disciple, Woman

Props: Table, Perfume bottle, and long-haired wig for the woman

Narrator: A woman anoints Jesus. "And being in Bethany in the house of Simon, the leper, as he sat at meat, there came a woman having an alabaster box of ointment of spikenard very precious; and she brake the box, and poured it on his head" (Mark 14:3). There were some in the company that did not agree with the manner of Jesus' anointing by the woman. Jesus said that the woman anointed Him for His burial.

(Everyone gathers around at a dinner table.)

Jesus: Thank you, Simon, for the dinner.

Disciple: The meal was terrific!

Woman: (The woman enters the room. She opens the perfume. She pours it on Jesus' head. She washes His feet with her hair (Mark14:3).

Disciple: (With anger) Woman, you wasted this expensive oil! That oil could have been sold to help the poor! (Mark 14:4-5)

Jesus: Let her alone. She did someone good. You will always have the poor, but I will not always be here. She anointed my body for my burial. She will be remembered for this (Mark 14:6-9).

Woman: (She continues to anoint Jesus during the song.)

♫ *Pour the Oil*♫

Matthew 26:6-13; Mark 14:3-9; Luke 7:36-50; John 12:1-8.

As the woman poured oil, costly oil, she said not a mumbling word. As she came to Jesus, she poured the oil
From His head down to His feet.
The disciple said woman, you wasted the oil. You wasted it for no cause.
But when Jesus heard them refer to the oil, this is just what He said:
I've been anointed to die for you. The woman saw no waste.
She poured from my head to my feet.
The poor you have always but Me as your Savior,
I've been anointed to die for you. I've been anointed to die for you.

As the woman poured oil, costly oil, she said not a mumbling word.
As she came to Jesus, she poured the oil
From His head down to His feet.
The disciple said woman, you wasted the oil. You wasted it for no cause.
But when Jesus heard them refer to the oil, this is just what He said:
I've been anointed to die for you. The woman saw no waste.
She poured from My head to My feet.
The poor you have always but Me as your Savior,
I've been anointed to die for you. I've been anointed to die for you.

Pour the oil, the alabaster oil. Pour the oil, the alabaster oil.
Pour the oil, the alabaster oil. Pour the oil, the alabaster oil.
From my head to my feet Pour, pour it pour it on him, the alabaster oil
From my head to my feet Pour, pour it pour it on him, the alabaster oil
From my head to my feet Pour, pour it pour it on him, the alabaster oil
From my head to my feet Pour, pour it pour it on him, the alabaster oil
From my head to my feet

End of Part Three

Part Four: The Death, Burial, and Resurrection of Jesus

Mark 10-16

Characters: Jesus, Narrator, Disciples (three is good), Crowd, Chief Officials, Centurion, Mother of Jesus, and Angels

Props: Garden of Gethsemane, Cross, Crown of Thorns, Sponge, and Scarlet Robe

Jesus: (With great emphasis) "Behold, we go up to Jerusalem; and the Son of man shall be delivered unto the chief priests, and unto the scribes; and they shall condemn Him to death, and shall deliver Him to the Gentiles: And they shall mock Him, and shall scourge Him, and shall spit upon Him, and shall kill Him: and the third day He shall rise again" (Mark 10:33-34).

Narrator: James and John desired to sit on the right and left of Jesus in glory, but Jesus reminded them that the most incredible place to be is in a position of servanthood. In later days, those in Jerusalem experienced Jesus' grand entrance into the area on a donkey, which fulfilled Old Testament prophecy. Later in his ministry, Jesus said that one of His disciples would betray Him. This scene continues in the Garden of Gethsemane. The disciples fall asleep as Jesus talks with the Father.

Jesus: Sit while I pray (Mark 14:32c). Tarry and watch (Mark 14:34b)

(One by one, the disciples fall asleep.)

Jesus: (Praying) Abba, Father, all things are possible unto Thee; take away this cup from Me; nevertheless, not My will but Your will (Mark 14:36)

(Jesus sees the disciples sleeping, and everyone wakes up.)

Jesus: Simon, could you watch but one hour? Watch and pray. The spirit is ready, but the flesh is weak (Mark 14:37-38). (They fall asleep).

Jesus: (Praying) Abba, Father, all things are possible unto Thee; take away this cup from Me; nevertheless, not my will but Your will (Mark 14:39.)

Jesus: You are sleeping again (Mark 14:40). (Praying) Abba, Father, all things are possible unto Thee; take away this cup from Me; nevertheless, not My will but Your will (Mark 14:41)

Jesus: Rise up. (Everyone gets up.) My time of betrayal is here (Mark 14:42). (Everyone leaves.)

Narrator: Many betrayed Jesus, especially Judas Iscariot. Chief people presented Jesus before the high priest. One disciple, Simon Peter, denied Jesus three times. Elders, along with the whole council, gave Jesus before Pilate. The crowd shouted to release Barrabas, a robber, and crucify Jesus, an innocent man. Pilate listened to the crowd.
The Crowd: Crucify Him! Crucify Him! Crucify Him! (Mark 15:13). (Jesus enters on a cross. He wears a crown of thorns and a scarlet robe. The people watch Him as He hangs on the cross.)

Mother of Jesus: (She watches as Jesus hangs on the cross.)

Jesus: "My God, My God, why hast thou forsaken me?" (Mark 15:34c)

(Someone lifts a sponge to Jesus' mouth.) (Mark 15:36)

Jesus: "It is finished" (Mark 15:37)

Centurion: "Truly this man was the Son of God" (Mark 15:39c).
(They carry Jesus away.)
Narrator: Jesus died for the sins of the world. He fulfilled the elements of a perfect sacrifice for humankind's sins, but how will He rise after His death? When many of His friends and family arrived at the tomb, Jesus' body was not there. Where did He go?

(As soft music plays, the angels escort all cast members down the aisle to the altar. Jesus appears as all kneel at the altar. Everyone rejoices!)

Narrator: "Behold, the days come, saith the Lord, that I will make a new covenant with the house of Israel, and with the house of Judah" (Jeremiah 31:31). Jesus Christ solidified the future of the New Covenant by living, dying, rising, and ascending back to heaven according to the Scriptures. The Lord opened the gift of grace to all who believe in the sacrificial work of Jesus Christ by faith. Amen. We await His next appearance. Let us celebrate.

♫ Kingdom Kids ♫

Ephesians 4:7-11

We are kingdom kids, and we're here today to celebrate to celebrate.
We are kingdom kids, and we're here today to celebrate to celebrate.
The measure of the gift. The gift of Jesus. Grace He gave to us.
I have a measure. I will use my gift in the body of Christ.
I will serve the Lord all my life. (Repeat one time)

I will use it to perfect the Saints. I will use it for the ministry.
I will edify the body. I will give the Lord all of me. (Repeat once)
We are kingdom kids, and we're here today to celebrate.

The End